NATIONAL GEOGRAPHIC KiDS

AWESOME
Maths & English
AGE 3-5

Get awesome at Maths and English!

Explore some of the world's most amazing animals and exercise brain cells on the way!

Four wild adventures open up fascinating facts about different creatures and provide practice for Maths and English:

- Spot some of the creatures that can be found in **mountain ranges** while conquering the **Numbers** topics.
- Uncover animals that live in and among **trees** while picking a way through the **Counting** topics.
- Admire animals that can be found in **Africa** while working through the **Phonics** topics.
- Find creatures that live in **woodlands and grasslands** while breezing through the **Writing** topics.

Awesome adventures await… good luck, explorer!

Published by Collins
An imprint of HarperCollins*Publishers*
Westerhill Road
Bishopbriggs
Glasgow G64 2QT

In association with National Geographic Partners, LLC

NATIONAL GEOGRAPHIC and the Yellow Border Design are trademarks of the National Geographic Society, used under license.

First published 2020

Text copyright © 2020 HarperCollins*Publishers*. All Rights Reserved.

Design copyright © 2020 National Geographic Partners, LLC. All Rights Reserved.

ISBN: 978-0-00-838879-9

10 9 8 7 6 5 4 3

The contents of this publication are believed correct at the time of printing. Nevertheless the publisher can accept no responsibility for errors or omissions, changes in the detail given or for any expense or loss thereby caused.

HarperCollins does not warrant that any website mentioned in this title will be provided uninterrupted, that any website will be error free, that defects will be corrected, or that the website or the server that makes it available are free of viruses or bugs. For full terms and conditions please refer to the site terms provided on the website.

A catalogue record for this book is available from the British Library

Printed in India by Multivista Global Pvt. Ltd.

If you would like to comment on any aspect of this book, please contact us at the above address or online.

natgeokidsbooks.co.uk

collins.reference@harpercollins.co.uk

Acknowledgements
P67, @ clipart.com; P78, © robertharding / Alamy Stock Photo
All other images are ©Shutterstock.com and ©HarperCollins*Publishers*

Author: Carol Medcalf
Publisher: Michelle I'Anson
Project Manager: Richard Toms
Cover Design: Sarah Duxbury
Inside Concept Design: Ian Wrigley
Page Layout: Ian Wrigley and Rose and Thorn Creative Services Ltd

MIX
Paper from responsible source
FSC® C007454

This book is produced from independently certified FSC™ paper to ensure responsible forest management.

For more information visit:
www.harpercollins.co.uk/green

Features of this book

Practice Tasks – activities to build confidence and improve skills

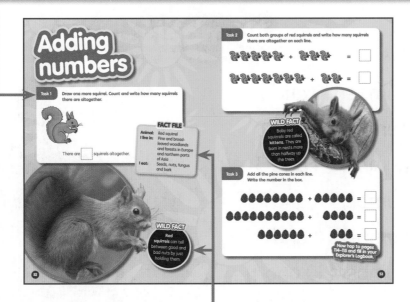

Wild Facts and Fact Files – weird, funny and interesting animal facts

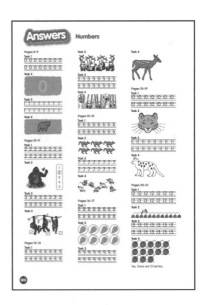

Explorer's Logbook – a tracker to record progress

Answers – the solutions to all the activities are at the back of the book

A certificate (see back page) rewards completion of the book.

Contents

Numbers

Counting

Phonics

Writing

The numbers 0 and 1

FACT FILE

Animal:	Brown bear
I live in:	Forests and mountains in North America, Scandinavia, Eastern Europe, Russia and China
I eat:	Meat, plants and honey

Task 1   Start at the red dot. Follow the arrows to trace the shape of the number **0** (zero). Then practise writing some on your own.

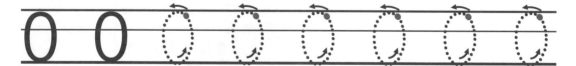

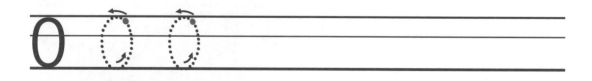

Task 2

There are no brown bears in this field. Say 'zero'. Now colour in the **0**.

0

WILD FACT

An adult brown bear can catch a jumping fish in its mouth!

Task 3

Start at the red dot. Follow the arrow to trace the shape of the number **1**. Then practise writing some on your own.

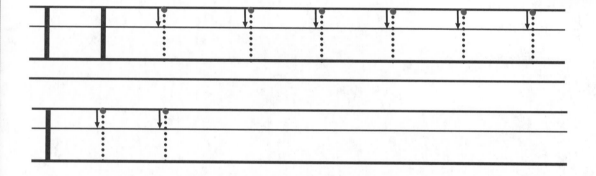

Task 4

There is **1** brown bear in this field. Colour in the bear.

Now make your way to pages 112–113 and fill in your Explorer's Logbook.

The numbers 2 and 3

FACT FILE

Animal:	Mountain gorilla
I live in:	Thick forests and rainforests in parts of Africa
I eat:	Plants, like wild celery, stinging nettles and bamboo

WILD FACT

Male gorillas are called **silverbacks,** as the hairs on their back are silver.

Task 1

Start at the red dot. Follow the arrows to trace the shape of the number **2**. Then practise writing some on your own.

2 2 2 2 2 2 2 2

2 2 2

Task 2

Circle the number to show how many plants the mountain gorilla is holding.

1
2
3
4
5

WILD FACT

Mother gorillas often carry their young ones on their back.

Task 3

Start at the red dot. Follow the arrows to trace the shape of the number **3**. Then practise writing some on your own.

Task 4

There are **3** baby mountain gorillas in the picture. Tick (✓) the boxes as you count to **3**.

Now swing to pages 112–113 and fill in your Explorer's Logbook.

11

The numbers 4 and 5

Start at the red dot (1). Follow the arrows to trace the shape of the number 4. Then practise writing some on your own.

4 4 4 4 4 4 4 4

4 4 4

FACT FILE

Animal: Giant panda
I live in: Forests in mountain ranges in central China
I eat: Bamboo

WILD FACT

Giant pandas are big eaters! They can munch through 12 kg of **bamboo** a day.

Task 2

There are 4 giant pandas in this picture. Colour them in.

Task 3

Start at the red dot (1). Follow the arrows to trace the shape of the number 5. Then practise writing some on your own.

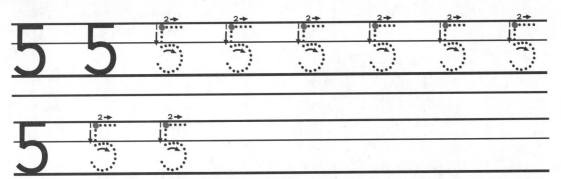

Task 4

Find and circle 5 giant pandas.

Now clamber to pages 112–113 and fill in your Explorer's Logbook.

The numbers 6 and 7

FACT FILE

Animal: Coyote
I live in: Forests, grassland, desert, scrubland and mountains in North and Central America
I eat: Rabbits, mice, insects, lizards and fruit

WILD FACT

Coyotes often work in **pairs** or small groups when **hunting** large animals.

| Task 1 | Start at the red dot. Follow the arrows to trace the shape of the number **6**. Then practise writing some on your own. |

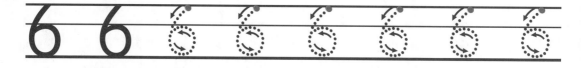

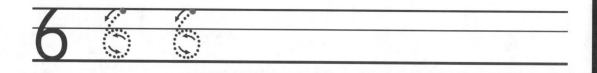

Task 2

Here are **6** coyotes. Count them and colour them in.

Task 3

Start at the red dot. Follow the arrows to trace the shape of the number 7. Then practise writing some on your own.

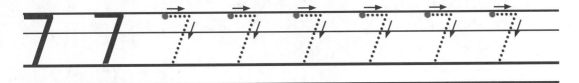

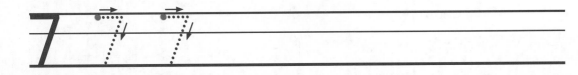

Task 4

Here are **7** mice hiding from a coyote. Draw a line to join them all together. Count 7.

WILD FACT

Coyotes raise a **litter** of 3 to 12 pups in **dens** or holes in the ground.

Now hunt down pages 112–113 and fill in your Explorer's Logbook.

15

The numbers 8 and 9

FACT FILE

Animal: Red deer
I live in: Woodlands, grasslands, moorland and river valleys in Europe and Western and Central Asia
I eat: Grasses, heather, leaves and twigs

WILD FACT

The **male red deer** is called a **stag**. He grows big **antlers** which fall off and regrow every year!

Task 1 Start at the red dot. Follow the arrows to trace the shape of the number 8. Then practise writing some on your own.

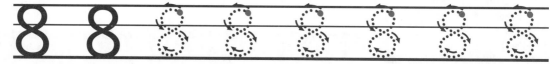

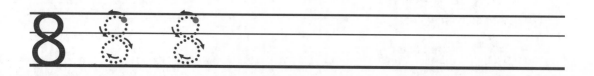

Task 2

There are **8** leaves. Circle each one as you count **8**.

Task 3

Start at the red dot. Follow the arrows to trace the shape of the number **9**. Then practise writing some on your own.

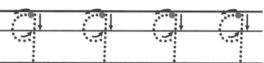

Task 4

Colour this deer. Leave its **9** spots in white.

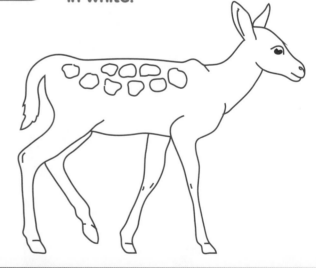

WILD FACT

Young red deer have white spots when they are born. The spots disappear as they grow up.

Now jump to pages 112–113 and fill in your Explorer's Logbook.

The numbers 10 and 11

Task 1

Start at the red dot. Follow the arrows to trace the shape of the number 10. Then practise writing some on your own.

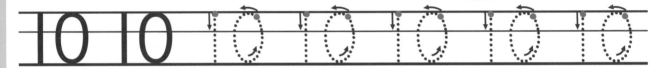

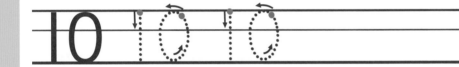

WILD FACT

Mountain lions often live by themselves.

18

Task 2

There are 10 whiskers on this mountain lion's face. Tick (✓) each one as you count to 10.

WILD FACT

Mountain lions can **leap** into a tree or climb over a fence that's higher than **a door!**

Task 3

Start at the red dot. Follow the arrows to trace the shape of the number 11. Then practise writing some on your own.

Task 4

Colour all 11 spots on this mountain lion cub.

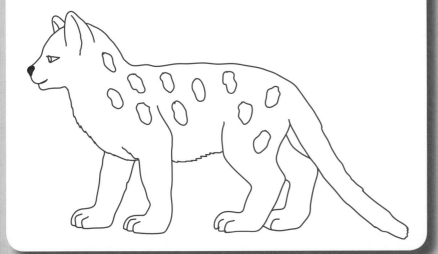

Now leap to pages 112–113 and fill in your Explorer's Logbook.

The numbers 12 and 13

FACT FILE

Animal: Arctic hare
I live in: Treeless mountain and coastal areas in the far north of Canada and Greenland
I eat: Plants, mosses, flowers, berries and bark

WILD FACT

In **winter**, **Arctic hares** have white fur which blends into the snow and helps them to avoid predators. In **summer** they are brown.

Task 1

Start at the red dot. Follow the arrows to trace the shape of the number 12. Then practise writing some on your own.

12 12 12 12 12 12

12 12 12

Task 2

This Arctic hare is jumping from rock to rock. Draw a line to join and count each rock. Did you count 12?

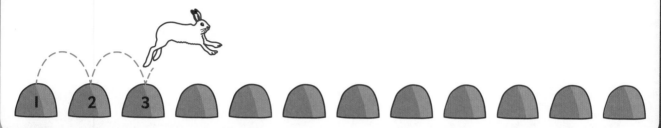

Task 3

Start at the red dot. Follow the arrows to trace the shape of the number 13. Then practise writing some on your own.

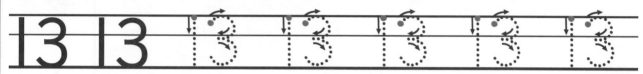

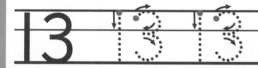

WILD FACT

Arctic **hares** have big **back feet** that stop them from **sinking** into the snow.

Task 4

Cross out each berry as you count them. Are there 13 berries in the picture?

Now hop to pages 112–113 and fill in your Explorer's Logbook.

21

The numbers 14 and 15

WILD FACT

Golden **eagles** build big **nests**, high on a cliff or tree. They are called **eyries**.

FACT FILE

Animal:	Golden eagle
I live in:	Open, natural habitats in North America, Europe and Asia
I eat:	Birds and animals such as deer and rabbits

Task 1 Start at the red dot. Follow the arrows to trace the shape of the number 14. Then practise writing some on your own.

14 14 14 14 14 14 14

14 14 14

Task 2

How many golden eagle eggs can you see? Count each one.

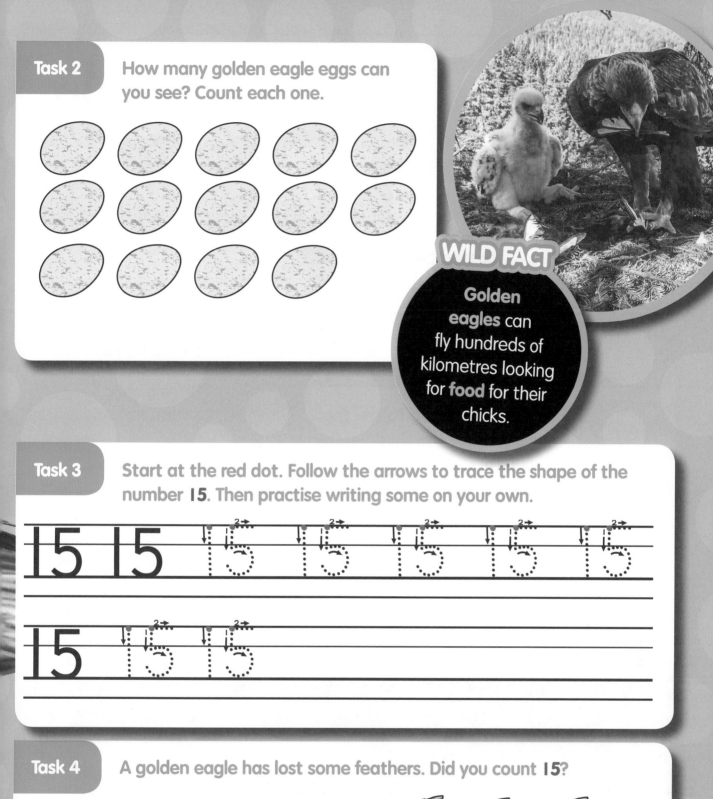

WILD FACT

Golden eagles can fly hundreds of kilometres looking for **food** for their chicks.

Task 3

Start at the red dot. Follow the arrows to trace the shape of the number **15**. Then practise writing some on your own.

15 15 15 15 15 15 15

15 15 15

Task 4

A golden eagle has lost some feathers. Did you count **15**?

Now glide to pages 112–113 and fill in your Explorer's Logbook.

The numbers 16 and 17

Task 1 Start at the red dot. Follow the arrows to trace the shape of the number **16**. Then practise writing some on your own.

16 16 16 16 16 16 16

16 16 16

WILD FACT

Raccoons are brilliant climbers and can swim quickly, so they can **escape** in a flash after snatching food.

Task 2

Colour these nuts for the raccoon to eat.
Count the nuts. How many are there?

WILD FACT

Raccoons are very clever. Those living **in and around towns** are very **skilled** in opening rubbish bins!

Task 3

Start at the red dot. Follow the arrows to trace the shape of the number 17. Then practise writing some on your own.

17 17 17 17 17 17

17 17 17

Task 4

Draw lines to join the dots, giving the raccoon 17 whiskers.

Now scurry to pages 112–113 and fill in your Explorer's Logbook.

The numbers 18 and 19

FACT FILE

Animal: American pine marten

I live in: Woods and forests in North America

I eat: Mice, birds, eggs and mushrooms

WILD FACT

Pine martens are very good **climbers** and can easily get to the top of the **highest** trees.

Task 1	Start at the red dot. Follow the arrows to trace the shape of the number 18. Then practise writing some on your own.

18 18 18 18 18 18 18

18 18 18

Count the pine martens. Are there **18**?

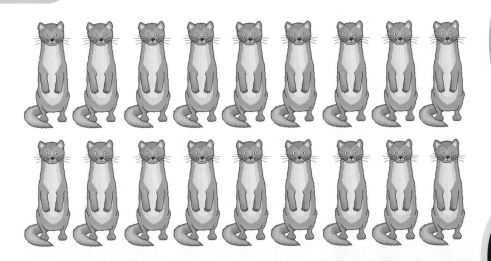

Task 3

Start at the red dot. Follow the arrows to trace the shape of the number **19**. Then practise writing some on your own.

19 19 19 19 19 19

19 19 19

Task 4

Colour the pine martens' tails. Count the tails. How many are there?

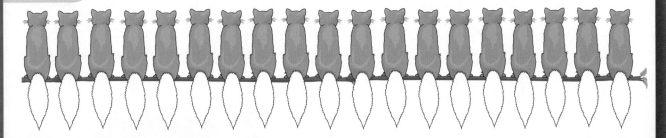

Now find pages 112–113 and fill in your Explorer's Logbook.

The number 20

Task 1

Start at the red dot. Follow the arrows to trace the shape of the number **20**. Then practise writing some on your own.

20 20 20 20 20 20 20

20 20 20

Task 2

Count the flowers that the pika will eat for dinner.
Are there **20**?

Task 3

Join the dots to find the pika.

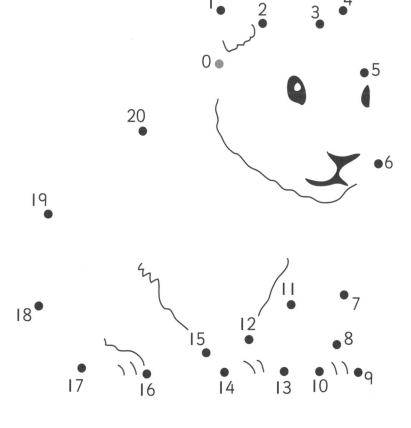

WILD FACT

Pikas bark to let each other know that **danger** is near.

Now scamper to pages 112–113 and fill in your Explorer's Logbook.

Number activities 0 to 20

FACT FILE

Animal:	Snow leopard
I live in:	Mountain ranges in Central Asia
I eat:	Sheep, goats, pikas and hares

Task 1	Follow the code to colour the picture.

1 = black
2 = blue
3 = brown
4 = green
5 = yellow

5

2

3

3

3

1

4

4

Task 2

Each of these snow leopards has a number from 6 to 10. Fill in the missing numbers.

WILD FACT

Snow leopards have very long tails which they **wrap** around their body to keep **warm.**

Task 3

Find and circle the hidden numbers.

Now race to pages 112–113 and fill in your Explorer's Logbook.

Recap writing 0 to 20

Practise writing the numbers 0 to 20. Start at the red dot. Follow the arrows to trace the shape of the number, then write your own underneath.

0   1   2

3   4   5

6   7   8

Count numbers 0, 1, 2

FACT FILE

Animal: Koala
I live in: Eucalyptus forests and open woodlands in eastern Australia
I eat: Eucalyptus leaves

WILD FACT

Koalas spend most of the time asleep!

| Task 1 | How many koalas are sitting in the trees? |

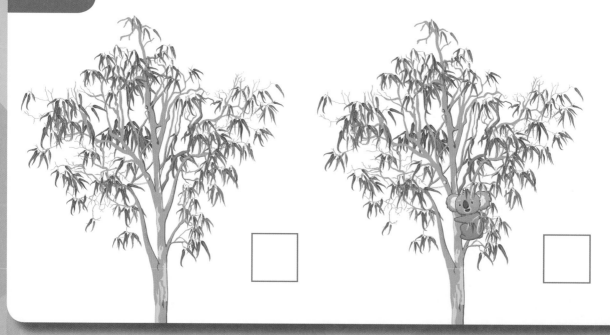

Look at the picture of the koala. Count how many eyes, ears, mouths and noses it has.

Eyes ☐   Ears ☐

Noses ☐   Mouths ☐

WILD FACT

A **baby koala** stays in its mummy's **pouch** for about 6 months. Once it leaves the pouch, it rides on her back or clings to her tummy. It goes **everywhere** with mum until it's about 1 year old.

Task 3

How many koalas can you see?

Circle the correct number.

0   1   2

Now climb to pages 114–115 and fill in your Explorer's Logbook.

Count numbers 3, 4, 5

FACT FILE

Animal: Leopard

I live in: Forests, mountains, grasslands and deserts in sub-Saharan Africa, north-east Africa, Central Asia, India and China

I eat: Deer, monkeys, fish and rodents

WILD FACT

Leopards are very good swimmers.

Task 1

The mother leopard has lost her **3** cubs. Can you draw a line to find them?

Task 2

Circle the leopard that has 4 pieces of meat.

WILD FACT

Leopards often **hunt** at night and **rest** in trees during the day.

Task 3

Draw a line to join the leopard with 5 spots to the big number 5.

5

Now creep to pages 114–115 and fill in your Explorer's Logbook.

Count numbers 6, 7, 8

Task 1

Colour **6** of these tree frogs.

WILD FACT

Some species, like the **squirrel tree frog,** can change colour.

Task 2

Circle **7** crickets for the tree frog to eat.

WILD FACT

Tree frogs have special tips on their toes to help them to **stick** to trees.

Task 3

Count the tree frogs in each group. Draw a line to the correct number.

6

7

8

Now hop to pages 114–115 and fill in your Explorer's Logbook.

Count numbers 9, 10, 11

Task 1   Colour 9 owls in each row.

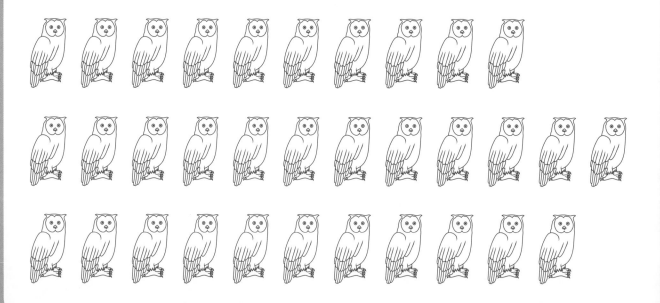

Task 2

Tick (✓) the box under the branch that has **10 baby owls** on it.

☐

☐

WILD FACT

Northern white-faced owls usually swallow their prey as one **whole** piece.

WILD FACT

When under **threat**, the northern white-faced owl makes a squeaky **growl**.

Task 3

Join the set that has **11 mice** in it to the big number 11.

11

Now swoop to pages 114–115 and fill in your Explorer's Logbook.

Count numbers 12, 13, 14

WILD FACT

The green tree python's head is **wider** than its body.

FACT FILE

Animal:	Green tree python
I live in:	Tropical rainforests such as those in New Guinea, the Solomon Islands and islands in Indonesia
I eat:	Mice and other small animals

Task 1 Count the groups and circle the correct number.

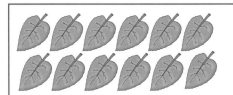   5   12   9

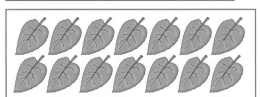   14   11   8

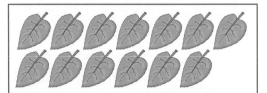   12   13   15

Task 2

How many times has the green tree python wrapped itself around the branch? Circle the correct answer.

12   13   14

WILD FACT

Green tree pythons spend much of their time wrapped over branches with their head resting on their body.

Task 3

Draw and colour 14 small patches in blue or yellow on the tree python. Then colour the snake green.

Now slither to pages 114–115 and fill in your Explorer's Logbook.

Count numbers 15, 16, 17

FACT FILE

Animal: Woodpecker
I live in: Woods and forests across most of the world
I eat: Insects, fruit, acorns and nuts

Task 1

Follow and count the numbers **0** to **15** to take the woodpecker to its nest.

2

1

7

10

0

6

13

3

9

11

4

8

5

12

14

15

44

Task 2 Find and circle the **16** woodpecker footprints.

WILD FACT

The **woodpecker's skull** is made of a spongy type of bone that **protects** its brain when it is drilling into a tree trunk.

Task 3 Count the number of nuts the woodpecker ate in a day. How many nuts are there?

Now land on pages 114–115 and fill in your Explorer's Logbook.

Count numbers 18, 19, 20

FACT FILE

Animal: Three-toed sloth
I live in: Tall trees in rain and cloud forests in Central and South America
I eat: Leaves and buds

WILD FACT

The **sloth** is the world's **slowest** mammal.

Task 1 Draw and colour **18** leaves on the tree for the sloth to eat.

Task 2

Count the leaves and circle the tree with **19** leaves.

Task 3

Tick (✓) the row that shows **20** raindrops.

⬭⬭⬭⬭⬭⬭⬭⬭⬭⬭⬭⬭⬭⬭⬭⬭⬭⬭   ☐

⬭⬭⬭⬭⬭⬭⬭⬭⬭⬭⬭⬭⬭⬭   ☐

⬭⬭⬭⬭⬭⬭⬭⬭⬭⬭⬭⬭⬭⬭⬭⬭⬭⬭⬭   ☐

⬭⬭⬭⬭⬭⬭⬭⬭⬭⬭⬭⬭⬭⬭⬭⬭⬭⬭⬭⬭   ☐

Now crawl to pages 114–115 and fill in your Explorer's Logbook.

Estimating and more or less

WILD FACT

An **orangutan's arms** are really long! They almost **touch the ground** when it is standing up!

Task 1

Estimate (guess) how many bananas the orangutan has picked. Don't count them – just look at the group and guess the number.

Task 2

Now count how many bananas there actually are in Task 1 and write the answer.

There are ☐ bananas.

Task 3

Colour the anthill that has more ants.

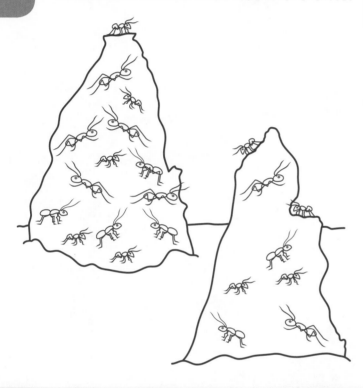

WILD FACT

When it rains, **orangutans** make **umbrellas** out of big leaves.

Task 4

The orangutans have found some pieces of durian fruit. Tick (✓) the group that has less.

Now swing to pages 114–115 and fill in your Explorer's Logbook.

Counting fun

WILD FACT

An **iguana** can **punch** an enemy with its tail to **defend** itself.

Task 1

Look at the picture. How many iguanas can you see? Colour them in.

I found ☐ iguanas.

Task 2

How many fruits are in each group? Count them and write the number in the box.

 ☐

 ☐

 ☐

 ☐

WILD FACT

Iguanas have very sharp claws to climb **trees,** but they are very good **swimmers** too.

Task 3

How many leaves can you see in each group? Count them and circle the correct number.

12   15   19

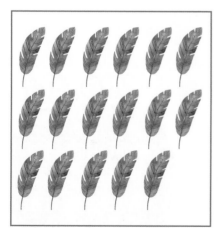

10   14   17

Now crawl to pages 114–115 and fill in your Explorer's Logbook.

51

Adding numbers

Task 1

Draw one more squirrel. Count and write how many squirrels there are altogether.

There are ☐ squirrels altogether.

FACT FILE

Animal: Red squirrel
I live in: Pine and broad-leaved woodlands and forests in Europe and northern parts of Asia
I eat: Seeds, nuts, fungus and bark

WILD FACT

Red **squirrels** can tell between good and bad nuts by just **holding** them.

Count both groups of red squirrels and write how many squirrels there are altogether on each line.

+ **=** ☐

+ **=** ☐

WILD FACT

Baby **red squirrels** are called **kittens.** They are born in nests more than halfway up the trees.

Task 3

Add all the pine cones in each line. Write the number in the box.

+ **=** ☐

+ **=** ☐

+ **=** ☐

Now hop to pages 114–115 and fill in your Explorer's Logbook.

Taking away numbers

Animal: Squirrel monkey
I live in: Tropical forests and marshes in Central and South America
I eat: Fruit, leaves, nuts, insects, lizards and eggs

WILD FACT

Squirrel **monkeys** are one of the **smallest** kinds of monkey in the world.

Task 1

Count the monkeys. Cross out **2**. How many are left?

[ ] monkeys left.

Task 2

One squirrel monkey has taken some figs from a tree.
How many are left?

 take away = ☐

 take away   = ☐

 take away = ☐

WILD FACT

Squirrel monkeys use their long tails to **balance** when they run through the tree tops.

Task 3

Take away the second number of leaves from the first number.
Write the answer.

 take away = ☐

 take away = ☐

Now dash to pages 114–115 and fill in your Explorer's Logbook.

Counting practice

FACT FILE

Animal: Fruit bat
I live in: Trees and caves across Africa, Asia and Australia
I eat: Fruit juice and flower nectar

Task 1 Count the bats and draw a line to match the group to the right number.

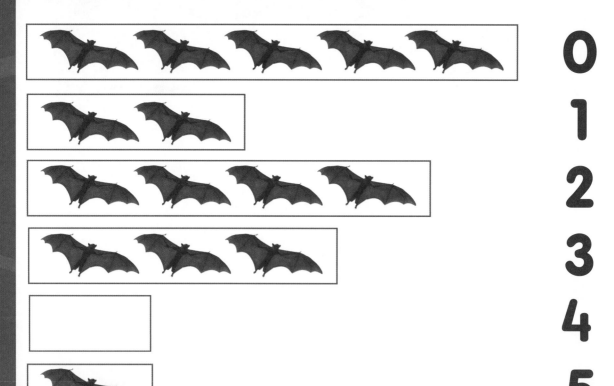

0
1
2
3
4
5

Task 2 How many cherries are there? Write the correct number in the box.

 ☐

 ☐

WILD FACT

To keep warm, **fruit bats** wrap themselves in their wings.

WILD FACT

While it is still small, a **baby fruit bat** stays with its **mother,** even when she is out hunting.

Task 3 Circle the correct number of melon slices for each set.

11   12

9   15

14   17

Now glide to pages 114–115 and fill in your Explorer's Logbook.

Recap numbers

Count the pictures in each set. Draw lines to match the set with the correct number. The number 0 has been done for you.

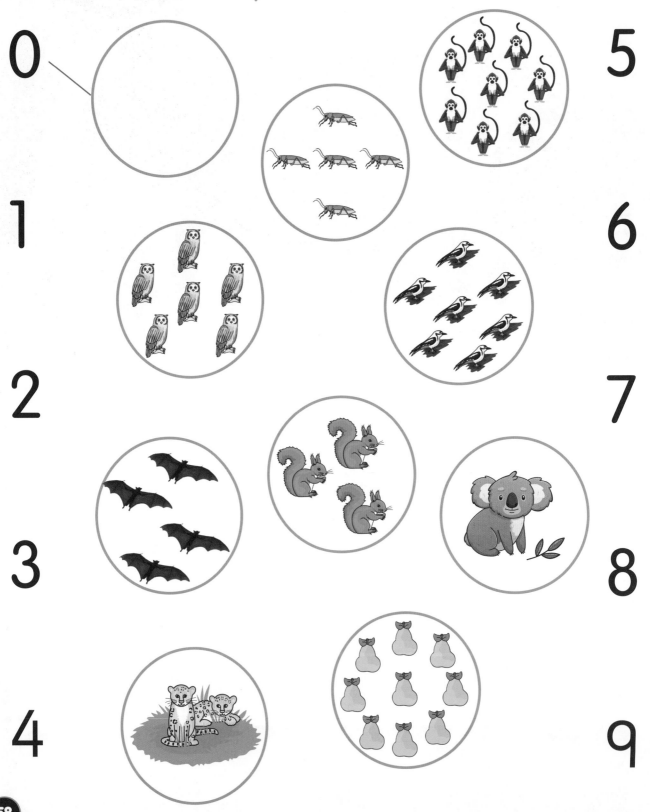

0

5

1

6

2

7

3

8

4

9

10

11

12

13

14

15

16

17

18

19

20

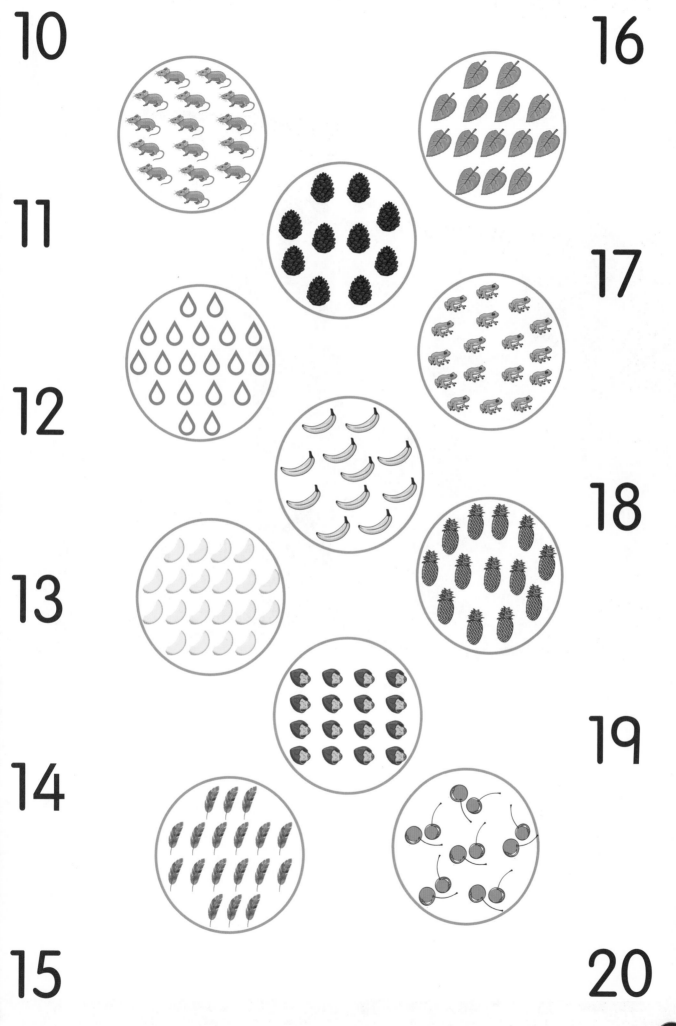

Phonic sounds
s and a

WILD FACT

Snakes can't chew their food, so they **swallow** things whole.

Task 1 Say the word for each picture. If it starts with **s**, draw a line to the letter **s**.

  S

Say the word for each picture. If it starts with **a**, draw a line to the letter **a**.

a

WILD FACT

Snakes **smell** things with their **tongue**!

Say the word for each picture. Circle the letter that matches the sound it starts with.

s p e u

m t a v

Now slither to pages 116–117 and fill in your Explorer's Logbook.

Phonic sounds t and p

FACT FILE

Animal: African penguin
I live in: The sea and on islands in South Africa and Namibia
I eat: Fish, squid and krill (small creatures found in the ocean)

Task 1	Say the word for each picture. Write **t** or **p** to start the word.

   _anda

   _iger

   _ortoise

   _enguin

Task 2

Say the word for each picture. Circle the letter for the sound it starts with.

 c b t z

 a p f j

WILD FACT

Penguins don't use their wings to fly through the air. Instead, they use them to **dart** through the water.

WILD FACT

Penguins have very heavy **bones** which help them **dive** through the water.

Task 3

Say the word for each picture. Draw lines to match it to the letter it starts with, **t** or **p**.

t

p

Now swim to pages 116–117 and fill in your Explorer's Logbook.

Phonic sounds i and n

Task 1

Join each letter i to a picture. They all start with the same i sound.

i   i   i

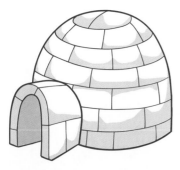      

Task 2   Say the word for each picture. Cross out the pictures that <u>do not</u> start with **n**.

q

WILD FACT

Young **impalas** join a group of other young impalas, where they **learn** to groom, move as a herd and play.

Task 3   Say the word. Listen to the sounds. Circle the sound of the red letter.

sun		s
bin		i
tap		p
ten	10	n

Now leap to pages 116–117 and fill in your Explorer's Logbook.

Phonic sounds m and d

| Task 1 | Say the word for each animal. Listen to the sound it starts with. Join it to the letter. |

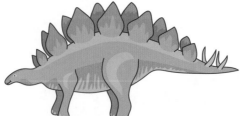

66

Task 2 Say the word for each picture.
Colour the pictures that start with m.

WILD FACT
When a **meerkat** stands up, it uses its **tail** to help it balance.

Task 3 Say the word for each picture. Circle the pictures that start with d.

Now scurry to pages 116–117 and fill in your Explorer's Logbook.

Phonic sounds g and o

FACT FILE

Animal: Giraffe
I live in: Savannahs and open woodlands of Africa
I eat: Leaves of the acacia tree

WILD FACT

Giraffes only eat the best **juicy leaves** and spit out thorns and tough twigs.

Task 1   Colour all the things in the picture that start with g.

68

Task 2

Say the word for each picture. Listen to the first sound. Cross out the one that <u>does not</u> start with o.

WILD FACT
Giraffes are the **tallest** animals in the world.

Task 3

Circle the picture that starts with the sound of the letter.

g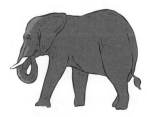

o

Now stroll to pages 116–117 and fill in your Explorer's Logbook.

Phonic sounds c, k and ck

FACT FILE

Animal: Crocodile
I live in: Rivers, lakes and swamps in North, Central and South America, Africa, Asia and Australia
I eat: Rats, snakes, antelopes, zebras, birds, fish and turtles

WILD FACT

Saltwater crocodiles are the largest reptiles in the world.

Task 1

Help the explorer to cross the crocodile river.
Colour all the stones that have pictures of things that start with c.

Task 2

Say the word for each picture. If it starts with the k sound, join it to the letter k.

WILD FACT

After baby crocodiles **hatch** out of the eggs, their mothers **carry them** to the water in their **mouths!**

Task 3

Say the word for each picture. Circle the ck sound.

clock

duck

black

chick

Now sneak to pages 116–117 and fill in your Explorer's Logbook.

Phonic sounds e and u

FACT FILE

Animal: African elephant
I live in: Floodplains, savannahs and woodlands of Africa
I eat: Grasses, fruit, roots, shrubs, leaves and bark

Task 1 Say the word for each picture. Colour the pictures that start with **e**.

WILD FACT

Elephants take care of each other. If one is **sick**, the others will look after it.

Task 2

Give each elephant a colourful umbrella and practise saying the **u** sound.

WILD FACT

An **elephant** uses its **trunk** for **picking up** and **pulling down** things and for sucking up water to put into its **mouth**.

Task 3

Write **e** or **u** to start each word. Say the words. Listen to the letter sounds.

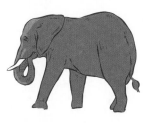   

_lephant _mbrella _gg _p

Now stride to pages 116–117 and fill in your Explorer's Logbook.

Phonic sounds
r, h and b

Task 1	Say the word for each picture. Listen to the first sound. Cross out the picture that <u>does not</u> start with r.

Say the word for each picture. Listen to the first sound. Circle the picture in each row that <u>does not</u> start with **h**.

h

h

Say the word for each picture. Draw lines from the letter **b** to the pictures that begin with **b**.

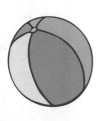  

WILD FACT

If their water **dries** up, **rhinoceros** dig for it with their **front** feet.

Now charge over to pages 116–117 and fill in your Explorer's Logbook.

Phonic sounds f, ff, l and ll

FACT FILE

Animal: Lion
I live in: Open plains, bush, woodlands and deserts in regions of Africa south of the Sahara
I eat: Buffalo, wildebeest and zebra

Task 1 Follow the maze to find the fox. Follow only the things that begin with the **f** sound.

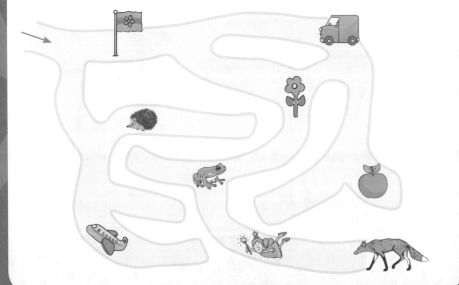

76

Task 2

Colour all these things. They all begin with the **l** sound.

 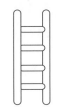 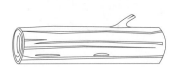

Task 3

Say the word for each picture. Write the **ff** sound in each word. Say the words and listen to the **ff** sound.

co__ee   cu__   to__ee

Task 4

Write **ll** at the end of each word. Say the words. Listen to the **ll** sound.

be__   she__   ta__   sma__

Now hunt down pages 116–117 and fill in your Explorer's Logbook.

Phonic sounds j, v and w

Task 1   Say the word for each picture. Circle the sound it begins with.

   q   n   j   w

   j   h   o   s

78

Task 2

Write **v** to start each word. Say the word. Listen to the letter sound **v**.

__olcano

__iolin

__ase

__egetables

Task 3

Tick (✓) the pictures that start with the **w** sound.

Now find your way to pages 116–117 and fill in your Explorer's Logbook.

Phonic sounds x, y, z and qu

FACT FILE

Animal: Zebra
I live in: Savannahs, grasslands, open woodlands and mountains mainly in eastern and southern parts of Africa
I eat: Grass, leaves, bark, flowers and fruits

Task 1 Say the word for each picture. Listen to the **x** sound. Circle the **x** sound in the words.

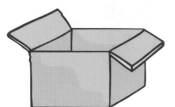

box

6

six

axe

x-ray

WILD FACT

Zebras can see in the dark much better than us.

Task 2 Say the word for each picture. Draw lines from the letter y to the pictures that begin with y.

WILD FACT

It is thought that a **mother zebra** can tell which **baby (foal)** is hers just by looking at its stripes.

Task 3 Draw lots of z letters on the zebra. Say the z sound.

Task 4 Colour each quarter of the zebra's patch a different colour. Practise saying the qu sound.

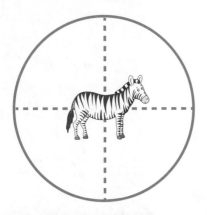

Now trot to pages 116–117 and fill in your Explorer's Logbook.

Reading words

FACT FILE

Animal: Hippopotamus
I live in: Grasslands in eastern, western and southern Africa where there is water and mud to wallow in
I eat: Grass and the remains of other animals

Task 1 Read the words. Draw a line to match each word to its picture.

bus

cap

net

bin

cot

WILD FACT

Hippos spend most of the day in the **water.** They come out to **eat** at **night.**

82

Task 2   Read the words. Draw a line to match the words that are the same.

am   is

at

in   in

is

am   at

WILD FACT

Hippos can open their mouths very wide! They do this to scare away other animals.

Task 3   Match each animal to its own food bowl.

 cat    dog    rat    bird

Now plod to pages 116–117 and fill in your Explorer's Logbook.

Practise phonic sounds

Can you remember all the sounds? Match each sound to the picture that starts with that sound.

a  g

p n

s  d

t  c

m  k

i  o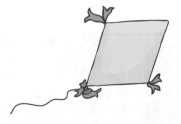

r   x

h   j

e   y

f   v

l   w

u   qu

b   z

Straight and wavy lines

FACT FILE

Animal: Fallow deer
I live in: Woodlands and grasslands mainly in Europe
I eat: Grasses and plants

Task 1 Colour the picture.

WILD FACT

Male fallow deer are called **bucks**. They fight one another using sharp horns on their heads, called **antlers**.

Task 2

Join the dots to lead the mother deer to their fawns.

WILD FACT

Baby fallow deer are called fawns and can walk within an hour of being born!

Task 3

Join the dots so the deer can jump over the fences to reach the wood.

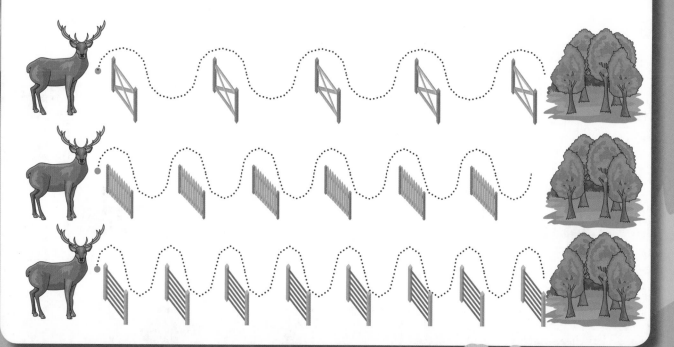

Now leap to pages 118–119 and fill in your Explorer's Logbook.

Patterns

FACT FILE

Animal: Hedgehog
I live in: Woodlands, parks and gardens widely in Europe, Asia and Africa
I eat: Insects, worms, snails and eggs

Task 1   Use your pencil to follow the pattern that the hedgehog has made in the leaves.

Task 2 Draw a nose, paws and spines on each hedgehog by joining the dots on the pictures.

WILD FACT

A **baby hedgehog** is called a **hoglet**.

Task 3 Follow the numbers to join the dots.

WILD FACT

To **protect** itself, a **hedgehog** will roll up into a **ball** with its sharp spines **sticking out.**

6   8   10
4   7
5
2   9
3
1

Now sneak to pages 118–119 and fill in your Explorer's Logbook.

Letters c, o and a

FACT FILE

Animal: Mole
I live in: A burrow under the ground in Europe, North America and Asia
I eat: Worms, ants, spiders and grubs

Task 1

Start at the red dot.
Follow the arrow to trace
the shape of the letter **c** with your pencil.
Then try some on your own.

WILD FACT

Moles have **two** thumbs on each paw.

Task 2

Start at the red dot. Follow the arrows to trace the shape of the letter **o**. Then write some on your own.

o o o o o

o o

WILD FACT

Moles can't **see** very well, so they use their **brilliant sense of smell** to find worms and insects.

Task 3

Start at the red dot. Follow the arrows to trace the shape of the letter **a**. Then try some on your own.

a a a a a

a a

Now dig out pages 118–119 and fill in your Explorer's Logbook.

Letters d and g

FACT FILE

Animal: Groundhog
I live in: Open country and woodland edges across Canada and in the United States
I eat: Plants, grasses and insects

WILD FACT

Groundhogs **sleep** all winter and **wake up** in spring.

Task 1

Start at the red dot. Follow the arrows to trace the shape of the letter **d**. Then try some on your own.

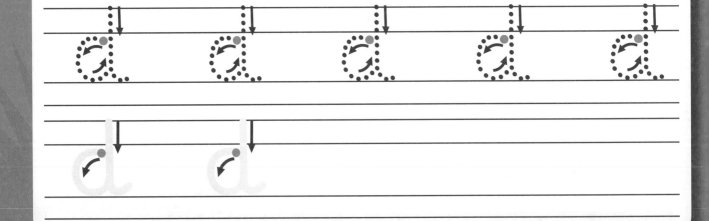

Task 2

 Start at the red dot. Follow the arrows to trace the shape of the letter **g**. Then try some on your own.

g g g g g

g g

WILD FACT

Groundhogs sometimes make a short whistling sound, so they are also called 'whistle-pigs'.

Task 3   Write **d** or **g** to finish these words.

red   log

peg   dog

Now burrow to pages 118–119 and fill in your Explorer's Logbook.

Letters i and r

Task 1

i↓

Start at the red dot (1). Follow the arrows to trace the shape of the letter i. Then try some on your own.

Animal:	Skunk
I live in:	Woodland, grasslands and towns in North and South America
I eat:	Insects, worms, rodents, frogs, birds, eggs, berries, roots, leaves, grasses and nuts

2● i↓   2● i↓   2● i↓   2● i↓   2● i↓

● i↓   ● i↓

WILD FACT

When it is **scared**, a **skunk** squirts very **smelly liquid** from under its **tail**!

Task 2

 Start at the red dot. Follow the arrows to trace the shape of the letter r. Then try some on your own.

Task 3

Draw a line to join each letter to the words that start with the same letter.

 rhino

i

 ink

 red

r

 iguana

 invitation

 rabbit

WILD FACT

Some **skunks** do 'handstands' to warn predators not to approach!

Now rush to pages 118–119 and fill in your Explorer's Logbook.

Letters n and m

FACT FILE

Animal:	Aardvark
I live in:	Grassland, woodland and rainforest in Africa
I eat:	Termites and ants

Task 1

Start at the red dot. Follow the arrows to trace the shape of the letter **n**. Then try some on your own.

96

Start at the red dot. Follow the arrows to trace the shape of the letter **m**. Then try some on your own.

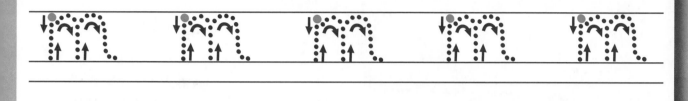

Task 3

Fill in the missing parts of each letter by joining the dots to finish each anthill.

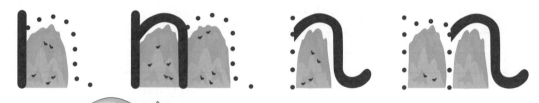

WILD FACT

Aardvarks can **close** their **nostrils** when eating so that ants don't climb up their noses!

Now dash to pages 118–119 and fill in your Explorer's Logbook.

Letters j, l and t

FACT FILE

Animal:	Wood mouse
I live in:	Woodland and fields in Europe and North Africa
I eat:	Plants, fruit, seeds and insects

Task 1

Start at the red dot (1). Follow the arrows to trace the shape of the letter j. Then try some on your own.

WILD FACT

Wood mice can use their **big back feet** to **leap** high into the air.

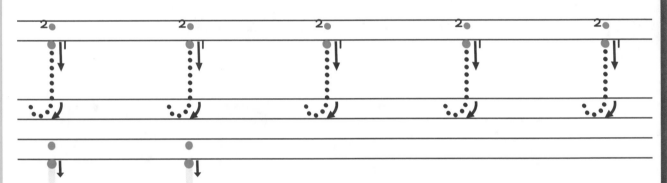

98

Task 2

Start at the red dot. Follow the arrow to trace the shape of the letter l. Then try some on your own.

WILD FACT

If it is caught by another animal, a **wood mouse** can **break off** the **end of its tail** to escape!

Task 3

Start at the red dot (1). Follow the arrows to trace the shape of the letter t. Then try some on your own.

Now scurry to pages 118–119 and fill in your Explorer's Logbook.

Letters h, k and f

FACT FILE

Animal: Rabbit
I live in: Woods, fields and meadows worldwide
I eat: Grass, flowers and farm crops

WILD FACT

Rabbits sometimes eat their own **poo!** This enables their body to get all the **nutrients** it needs.

Task 1

Start at the red dot. Follow the arrows to trace the shape of the letter h. Then try some on your own.

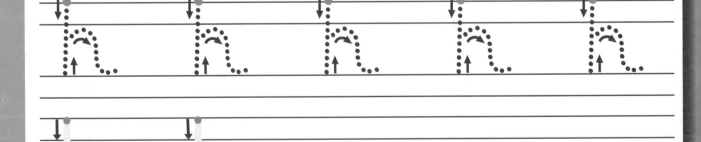

Task 2

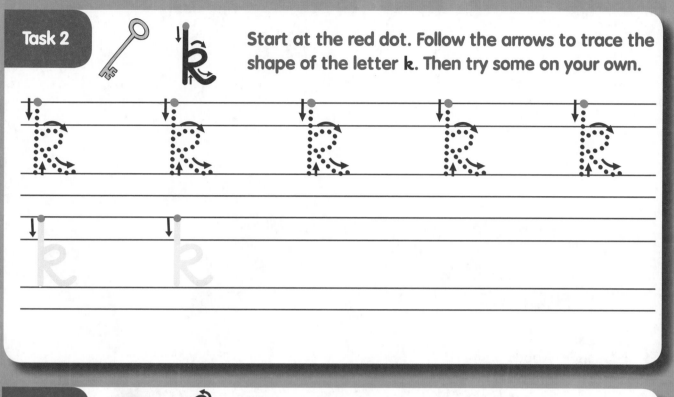

Start at the red dot. Follow the arrows to trace the shape of the letter k. Then try some on your own.

Task 3

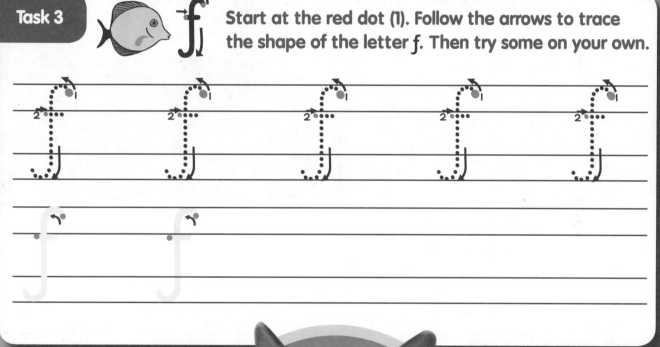

Start at the red dot (1). Follow the arrows to trace the shape of the letter f. Then try some on your own.

WILD FACT

Rabbits can see in almost all directions without even turning their heads.

Now hop to pages 118–119 and fill in your Explorer's Logbook.

Letters b, s and e

FACT FILE

Animal: Badger
I live in: Woods and grasslands across Europe, Asia, Africa and North America
I eat: Worms, insects, eggs, fruit and small animals

Task 1

Start at the red dot. Follow the arrows to trace the shape of the letter **b**. Then try some on your own.

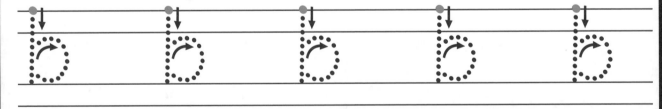

Task 2

Start at the red dot. Follow the arrows to trace the shape of the letter **s**. Then try some on your own.

WILD FACT

Badgers dig **burrows** with long tunnels and a large room for sleeping.

WILD FACT

A **badger** can **eat** hundreds of **worms** each night.

Task 3

Start at the red dot. Follow the arrows to trace the shape of the letter **e**. Then try some on your own.

Now run to pages 118–119 and fill in your Explorer's Logbook.

Letters q and p

Task 1

FACT FILE

Animal: Earthworm
I live in: The soil worldwide
I eat: Leaves and plant roots

Start at the red dot. Follow the arrows to trace the shape of the letter q. Then try some on your own.

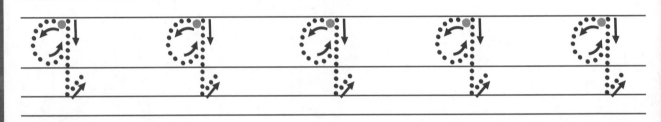

WILD FACT

Earthworms breathe through their skin!

104

Task 2

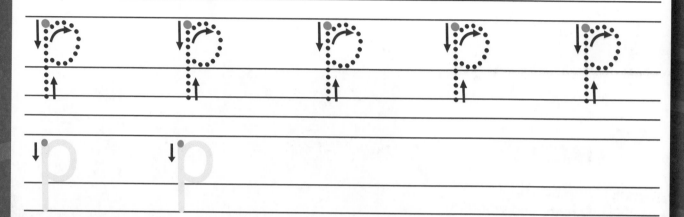

Start at the red dot. Follow the arrows to trace the shape of the letter **p**. Then try some on your own.

Task 3

Follow the maze to take the worm from its home up to the leaf. Find and colour in the letters **p** and **q**.

WILD FACT

Earthworms don't have any bones!

Now wriggle to pages 118–119 and fill in your Explorer's Logbook.

Letters y, u and v

FACT FILE

Animal: American black bear
I live in: Forests and woods in North America
I eat: Grasses, roots, berries and insects

WILD FACT

Black bears **sleep** all **winter** and don't go to the **toilet** at all during this time!

Task 1

  Start at the red dot. Follow the arrows to trace the shape of the letter **y**. Then try some on your own.

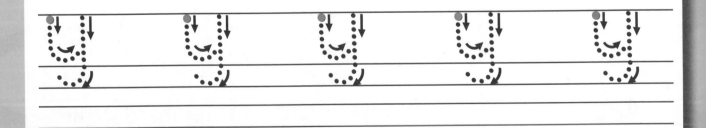

Task 2

u

Start at the red dot. Follow the arrows to trace the shape of the letter **u**. Then try some on your own.

WILD FACT

Black bears are very good at climbing trees.

Task 3

V

Start at the red dot. Follow the arrows to trace the shape of the letter **v**, then try some on your own.

Now climb to pages 118–119 and fill in your Explorer's Logbook.

Letters w, z and x

FACT FILE

Animal: Red fox
I live in: Woods, grasslands and towns across North America, Europe and Asia
I eat: Small animals, birds, beetles, fruit, insects and worms

Task 1

Start at the red dot. Follow the arrows to trace the shape of the letter w. Then try some on your own.

WILD FACT

A **fox** uses its **bushy tail** as a **blanket** to keep warm in winter.

Task 2

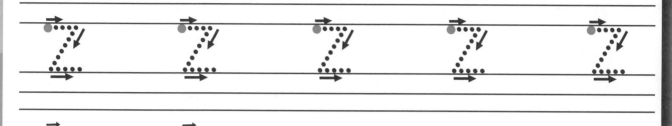

Start at the red dot. Follow the arrows to trace the shape of the letter **z**. Then try some on your own.

Z Z Z Z Z

Z Z

WILD FACT

Foxes use their excellent **hearing** to **hunt** for animals that they can't see but can hear moving around.

Task 3

Start at the red dot (1). Follow the arrows to trace the shape of the letter **x**. Then try some on your own.

X X X X X

X X

Now scamper to pages 118–119 and fill in your Explorer's Logbook.

Recap writing a-z

Practise writing the alphabet. Start at the red dot. Follow the arrows to trace the shape of the letter, then write your own underneath.

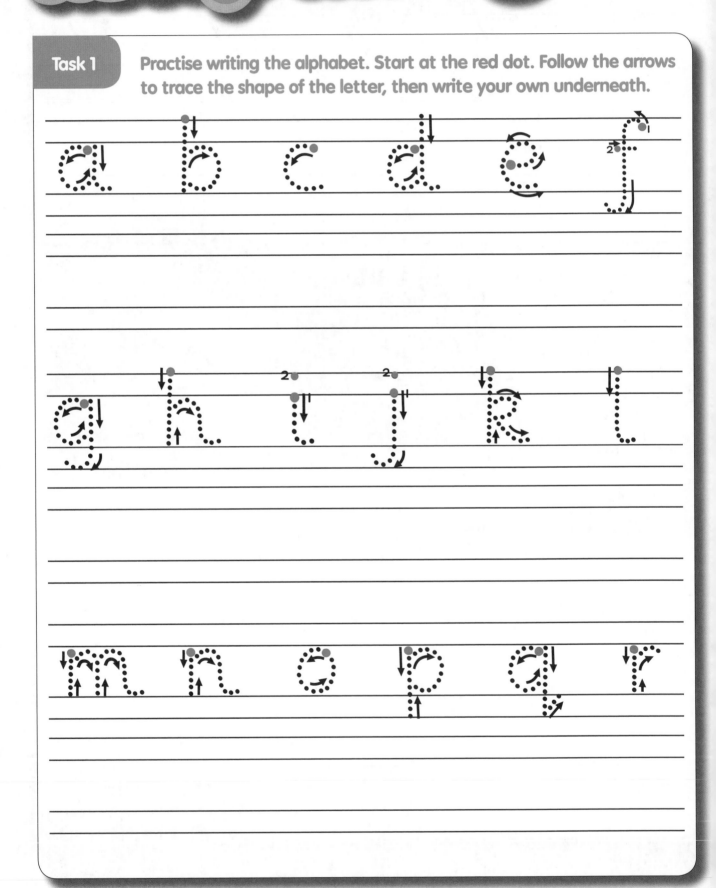

s t u v w x

y z

Task 2   Now you can write all the letters, can you write your own name here?

111

Explorer's Logbook

Numbers

Tick off the topics as you complete them and colour in the star to show how you feel.

The numbers
0 and 1 ☐

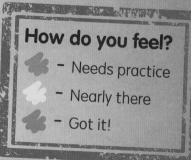

The numbers
2 and 3 ☐

The numbers
4 and 5 ☐

The numbers
6 and 7 ☐

The numbers
8 and 9 ☐

The numbers
10 and 11 ☐

The numbers
12 and 13 ☐

The numbers
14 and 15 ☐

The numbers
16 and 17 ☐

The numbers
18 and 19 ☐

The number 20 ☐

Number activities
0 to 20 ☐

Explorer's Logbook

Counting

Tick off the topics as you complete them and colour in the star to show how you feel.

Count numbers
0, 1, 2 ☐

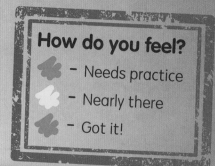

Count numbers
3, 4, 5 ☐

Count numbers
6, 7, 8 ☐

Count numbers
9, 10, 11 ☐

Count numbers
12, 13, 14 ☐

Count numbers
15, 16, 17 ☐

Count numbers
18, 19, 20 ☐

Estimating and more
or less ☐

Counting fun ☐

Adding numbers ☐

Taking away numbers ☐

Counting practice ☐

Explorer's Logbook

Phonics

Tick off the topics as you complete them and colour in the star to show how you feel.

Phonic sounds
s and a ☐

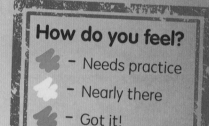

Phonic sounds
t and p ☐

Phonic sounds
i and n ☐

Phonic sounds
m and d ☐

Phonic sounds
g and o ☐

Phonic sounds e and u ☐

Phonic sounds
r, h and b ☐

Phonic sounds c, k
and ck ☐

Phonic sounds
x, y, z and qu ☐

Phonic sounds
j, v and w ☐

Phonic sounds f, ff, l
and ll ☐

Reading words ☐

117

Explorer's Logbook

Writing

Tick off the topics as you complete them and colour in the star to show how you feel.

Patterns ☐

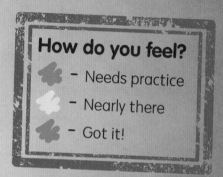
Straight and wavy lines ☐

Letters c, o and a ☐

Letters d and g ☐

Letters i and r ☐

Letters n and m ☐

Letters j, l and t ☐

Letters h, k and f ☐

Letters b, s and e ☐

Letters q and p ☐

Letters y, u and v ☐

Letters w, z and x ☐

 **Numbers**

Pages 8–9

Task 1

0 0 0 0 0 0 0 0

0 0 0 0 0 0 0 0

Task 2

Task 3

Task 4

Pages 10–11

Task 1

2 2 2 2 2 2 2 2

2 2 2 2 2 2 2 2

Task 2

1
② 2
3
4
5

Task 3

3 3 3 3 3 3 3 3

3 3 3 3 3 3 3 3

Task 4

✓   ✓   ✓

Pages 12–13

Task 1

4 4 4 4 4 4 4 4

4 4 4 4 4 4 4 4

Task 2

Task 3

5 5 5 5 5 5 5 5

5 5 5 5 5 5 5 5

Task 4

Pages 14–15

Task 1

6 6 6 6 6 6 6

6 6 6 6 6 6 6

Task 2

Task 3

7 7 7 7 7 7 7 7

7 7 7 7 7 7 7 7

Task 4

Pages 16–17

Task 1

8 8 8 8 8 8 8

8 8 8 8 8 8 8

Task 2

Task 3

9 9 9 9 9 9 9 9

9 9 9 9 9 9 9 9

Task 4

Pages 18–19

Task 1

10 10 10 10 10 10 10

10 10 10 10 10 10 10

Task 2

✓ ✓ ✓

Task 3

Task 4

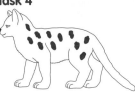

Pages 20–21

Task 1

12 12 12 12 12 12 12

12 12 12 12 12 12 12

Task 2

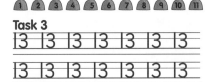

1 2 3 4 5 6 7 8 9 10 11 12

Task 3

13 13 13 13 13 13 13

13 13 13 13 13 13 13

Task 4

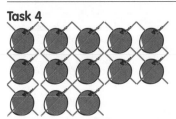

Yes, there are 13 berries.

Pages 22–23

Task 1

14	14	14	14	14	14	14
14	14	14	14	14	14	14

Task 2

There are 14 golden eagle eggs.

Task 3

15	15	15	15	15	15	15
15	15	15	15	15	15	15

Task 4

There are 15 golden eagle feathers.

Pages 24–25

Task 1

16	16	16	16	16	16	16
16	16	16	16	16	16	16

Task 2

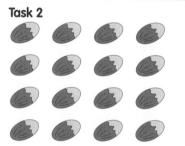

There are 16 nuts.

Task 3

17	17	17	17	17	17	17
17	17	17	17	17	17	17

Task 4

Pages 26–27

Task 1

18	18	18	18	18	18	18
18	18	18	18	18	18	18

Task 2

Yes, there are 18 pine martens.

Task 3

19	19	19	19	19	19	19
19	19	19	19	19	19	19

Task 4

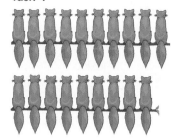

There are 19 tails.

Pages 28–29

Task 1

20	20	20	20	20	20	20
20	20	20	20	20	20	20

Task 2

Yes, there are 20 flowers for the pika to eat for dinner.

Task 3

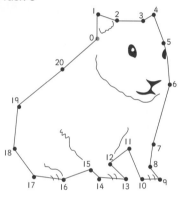

Pages 30–31

Task 1

Task 2

Task 3

Pages 32–33

0	1	2
0	1	2

3	4	5
3	4	5

6	7	8
6	7	8

9	10	11
9	10	11

12	13	14
12	13	14

15	16	17
15	16	17

18	19	20
18	19	20

 **Counting**

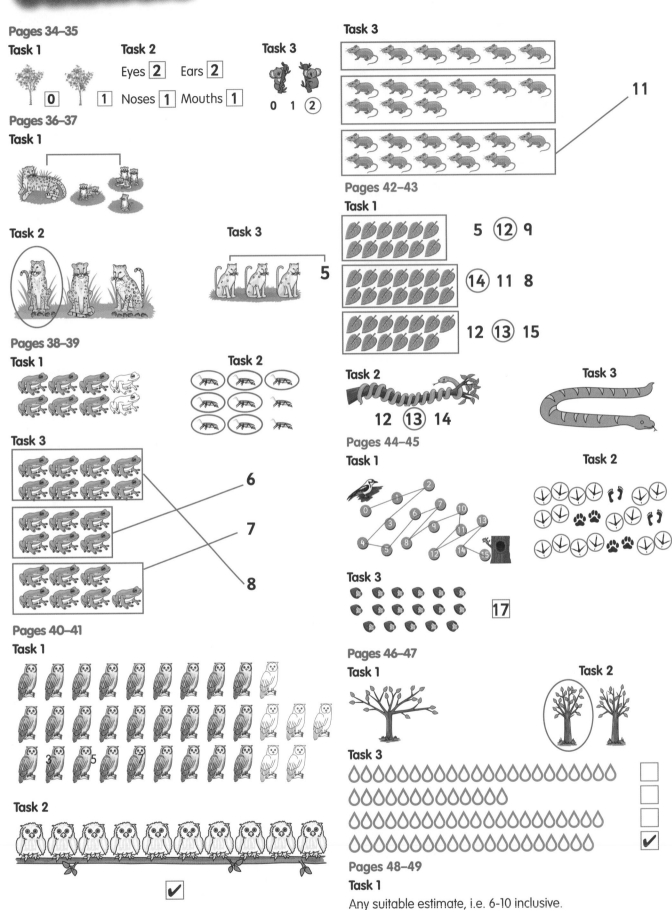

Pages 34–35

Task 1

0   1

Task 2

Eyes 2   Ears 2
Noses 1   Mouths 1

Task 3

0 1 ②

Pages 36–37

Task 1

Task 2

Task 3

5

Pages 38–39

Task 1

Task 2

Task 3

6

7

8

Pages 40–41

Task 1

3   5

Task 2

✓

Task 3

11

Pages 42–43

Task 1

5 ⑫ 9

⑭ 11 8

12 ⑬ 15

Task 2

12 ⑬ 14

Task 3

Pages 44–45

Task 1

Task 2

Task 3

17

Pages 46–47

Task 1

Task 2

Task 3

✓

Pages 48–49

Task 1

Any suitable estimate, i.e. 6-10 inclusive.

Task 2

There are 8 bananas.

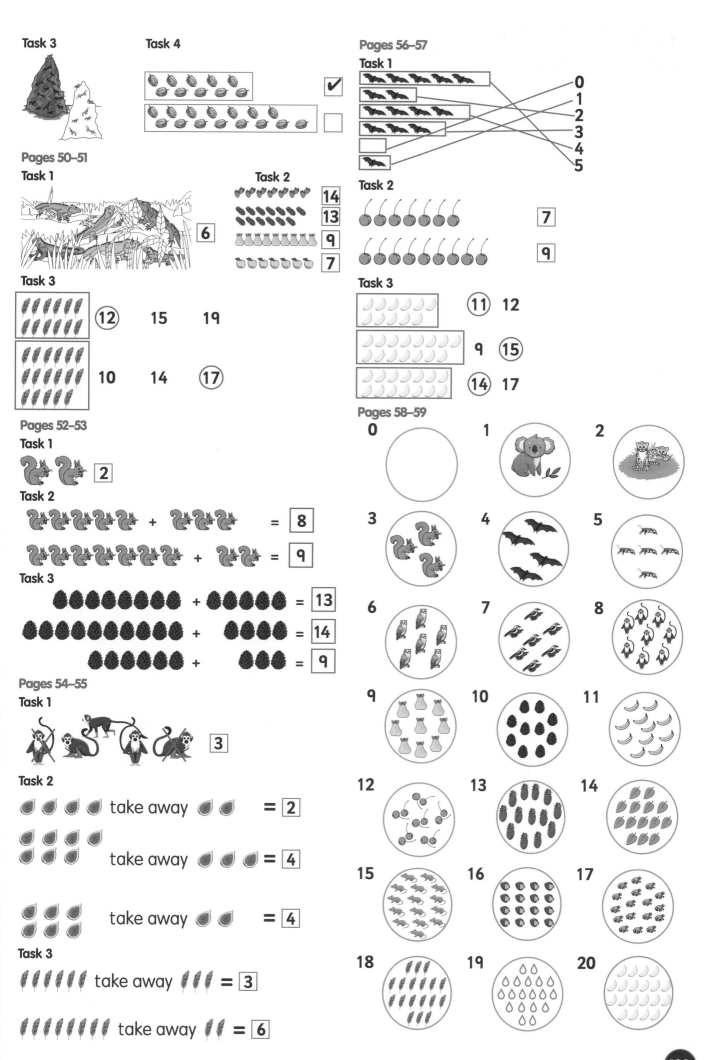

Task 3

Task 4

☑

☐

Pages 50–51

Task 1

6

Task 2

14
13
9
7

Task 3

⑫   15   19

10   14   ⑰

Pages 52–53

Task 1

2

Task 2

+ = 8

+ = 9

Task 3

+ = 13

+ = 14

+ = 9

Pages 54–55

Task 1

3

Task 2

take away = 2

take away = 4

take away = 4

Task 3

take away = 3

take away = 6

Pages 56–57

Task 1

0
1
2
3
4
5

Task 2

7

9

Task 3

⑪ 12

9 ⑮

⑭ 17

Pages 58–59

0

1

2

3

4

5

6

7

8

9

10

11

12

13

14

15

16

17

18

19

20

Answers   Phonics

Pages 60–61
Task 1

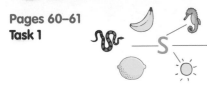

Task 2

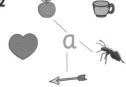

Task 3   (s)   p   e   u

m   t   (a)   v

Pages 62–63
Task 1   panda, tiger, tortoise, penguin

Task 2   c   b   (t)   z

a   (p)   f   j

Task 3

t   p

Pages 64–65
Task 1   i   i   i

Task 2

q

Task 3   (sun) (bin) (tap) (ten)

Pages 66–67
Task 1

m   d

Task 2

Task 3

Pages 68–69
Task 1

Task 2

Task 3 g

o

Pages 70–71
Task 1

Task 2

k

Task 3   clo(ck)   du(ck)   bla(ck)   chi(ck)

Pages 72–73
Task 1

Task 2

Task 3   **e**lephant   **u**mbrella   **e**gg   **u**p

Pages 74–75
Task 1

Task 2 h

h

Task 3
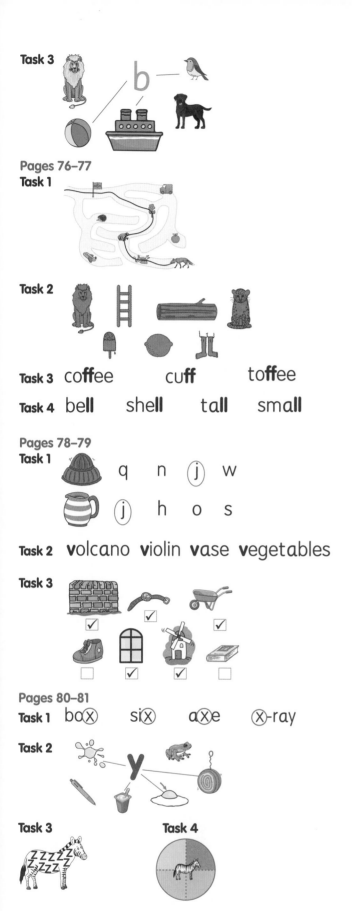

Pages 76–77

Task 1

Task 2

Task 3 co**ff**ee   cu**ff**   to**ff**ee

Task 4 be**ll**   she**ll**   ta**ll**   sma**ll**

Pages 78–79

Task 1 q   n   (j)   w

(j)   h   o   s

Task 2 **v**olcano   **v**iolin   **v**ase   **v**egetables

Task 3

☑   ☑

☐   ☑   ☑   ☐

Pages 80–81

Task 1 bo(x)   si(x)   a(x)e   (x)-ray

Task 2

Task 3

Task 4

Pages 82–83

Task 1

bus
cap
net
bin
cot

Task 2

am   is   at
in —— in   is
am   at

Task 3

Pages 84–85

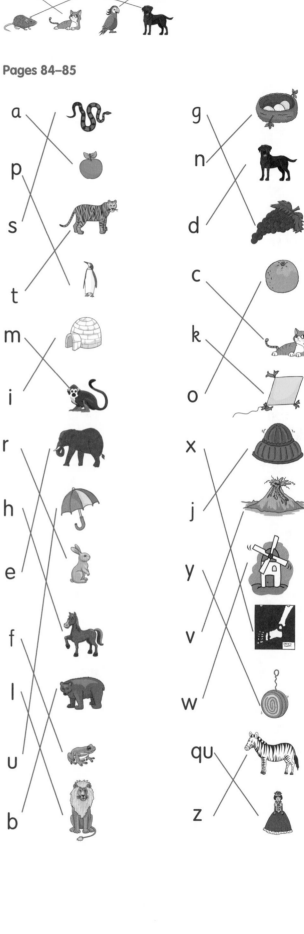

a   p   s   t   m   i   r   h   e   f   l   u   b

g   n   d   c   k   o   x   j   y   v   w   qu   z

Answers Writing

Pages 86–87

Task 1

Task 2

Task 3

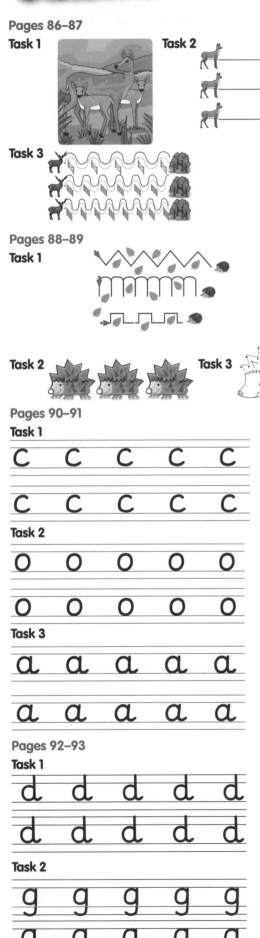

Pages 88–89

Task 1

Task 2

Task 3

Pages 90–91

Task 1

C C C C C
c c c c c

Task 2

O O O O O
O O O O O

Task 3

a a a a a
a a a a a

Pages 92–93

Task 1

d d d d d
d d d d d

Task 2

g g g g g
g g g g g

Task 3

red   log
peg   dog

Pages 94–95

Task 1

i i i i i
i i i i i

Task 2

r r r r r
r r r r r

Task 3

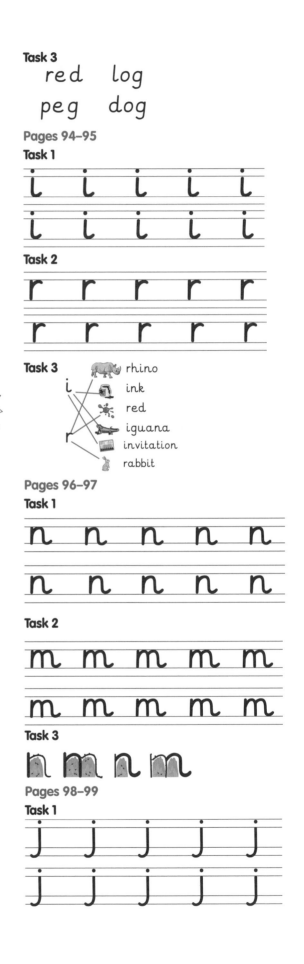

i ——— rhino
      ink
      red
      iguana
r ——— invitation
      rabbit

Pages 96–97

Task 1

n n n n n
n n n n n

Task 2

m m m m m
m m m m m

Task 3

n n m n m

Pages 98–99

Task 1

j j j j j
j j j j j

Task 2

t t t t t

t t t t t

Task 3

t t t t t

t t t t t

Pages 100–101

Task 1

h h h h h

h h h h h

Task 2

k k k k k

k k k k k

Task 3

f f f f f

f f f f f

Pages 102–103

Task 1

b b b b b

b b b b b

Task 2

s s s s s

s s s s s

Task 3

e e e e e

e e e e e

Pages 104–105

Task 1

q q q q q

q q q q q

Task 2

p p p p p

p p p p p

Task 3

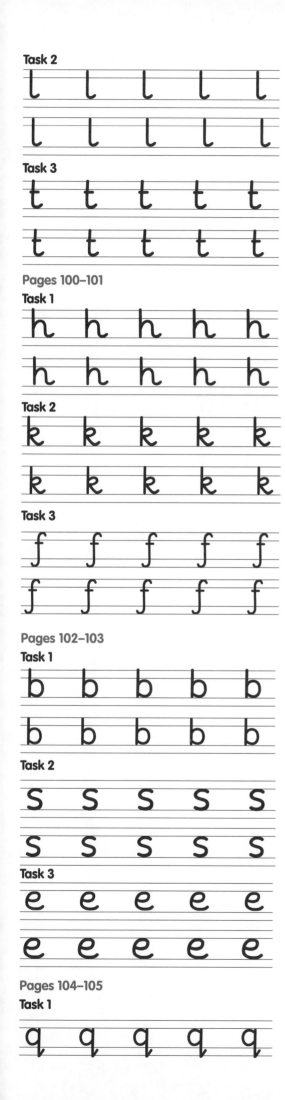

Pages 106–107

Task 1

y y y y y

y y y y y

Task 2

u u u u u

u u u u u

Task 3

v v v v v

v v v v v

Pages 108–109

Task 1

W W W W W

W W W W W

Task 2

Z Z Z Z Z

Z Z Z Z Z

Task 3

X X X X X

X X X X X

You're awesome!

Well done, you have finished your adventures

Explorer's pass

Name: _____

Age: _____

Date: _____

Draw a picture of yourself in the box!